Contemporary Crafts

Stencilling

KATHY FILLION RITCHIE

Contemporary Crafts

Stencilling

KATHY FILLION RITCHIE

TIGER BOOKS
INTERNATIONAL

First published in 1995 by
New Holland Publishers (UK) Ltd
London • Cape Town • Sydney • Singapore

24 Nutford Place
London W1H 6DQ
United Kingdom

80 McKenzie Street
Cape Town 8001
South Africa

3/2 Aquatic Drive
Frenchs Forest, NSW 2086
Australia

This edition published in 1998 by
Tiger Books International Plc, Twickenham, U.K.

ISBN 1 84056 017 7

Printed and bound in Singapore by Tien Wah Press (Pte) Ltd

2 4 6 8 10 9 7 5 3 1

Acknowledgments
The author and publishers would like to thank Stewart Walton,
Eleanor Allitt, Pavilion Originals, Alison at Infopress, The Stencil Store
and Aurum Press.

CONTENTS

INTRODUCTION

IN THE PAST FEW YEARS there has been increased interest in folk art, which includes the method of decorative painting called stencilling. The word stencilling probably originates from the French *estenceler* meaning to sparkle or cover with stars. This is a beautiful image to keep in the back of your mind as you consider the art of stencilling for yourself.

Technically, stencilling is a method of painting that involves applying paint, ink or dye through a pattern which has been cut from any material which is durable, and which allows you to reposition it and use it many times over. In the past, stencils were made out of leather or thin sheets of metal. Today, the most common stencils are made out of oiled card or clear plastic acetate. Stencilling can be thought of as a method of positive painting or printing. The image that is cut out is the image that you will see when the paint is applied.

It seems to be that towards the close of the 20th century we are looking for things that are not mass produced, but instead have character and history. Maybe we are looking for the authenticity that we can no longer find in shops. Maybe we are trying to put the 'roots' back into our surroundings. It seems to be that this trend has extended itself to the decorative arts.

There is a new interest in painted furnishings.

Your own personal orangery can be created with the aid of stencils and paint. This beautiful orange tree and the decorative pot in which it sits is available to buy as a pre-cut stencil.

. . . .

We find that a piece of furniture that is painted is being carefully considered before being altered in any way. Is it an original finish? Furniture sold at auction now brings a higher price if its original painted finish is still intact. In some instances, layers of paint are being carefully removed in an effort to reveal clues as to the original colour. There are now many paint companies that are reproducing the colours used by the Victorians or Colonial Americans, which can help when trying to 'restore' a piece to its original colour.

This desire to recycle objects and give them new life by careful hand painting can invest something of 'character' that was lacking before. It is your own personal touch, and therefore makes the piece unique.

When you design your own stencils you create patterns which are exactly the design and size that you want. They can also be painted in the colour of your choice. Stencilling is a way to be inspired about patterning without feeling daunted at the prospect of acually painting.

The recent documented history of stencilling began in the early nineteenth century. The discovery of the ruins of Pompei in the late 1700s shifted the focus of European decorative painting away from trompe l'oeil or highly illusionistic painting. In about 1800, the focus and indeed the fashion in decorative painting for home interiors became flat and two-dimensional. This new two-dimensional decoration relied on large areas of flat, rich colour which were usually plain, with bold borders. These borders would

be at baseboard, dado rail or ceiling height. Any embellishment within the borders took the form of relatively small, careful, repeated patterns executed in freehand painting or by stencilling. Stencilling allowed the painter to produce repeated patterns accurately and quickly.

This was the fashion in Europe of the wealthy which later trickled down to the less wealthy. Painting had always been a way for the populace to decorate and add colour to their simple, utilitarian furnishings without the expense of fabric or paper wallcoverings. As it was commonplace for walls, floors and floorcloths, furniture and accessories to be painted, stencilling was a way to add pattern simply and inexpensively. For example, fabrics such as bedspreads and tablecloths were stencilled as substitutes for more elaborate embroidered fabrics.

Car spray paint was applied directly to the aging, varnished finish of this old chest of drawers. The design shows intertwining bramble sprays and five tiny wrens hiding among the foliage. The beauty of this method of stencilling is that the natural wood finish is unobscured by the painted design.

. . . .

The painting of floorcloths is an early form of interior decoration that is once again becoming popular. These simple furnishings were used extensively in Europe and America from about 1650 to the end of the 19th century. They were made of heavy sailcloth, often recycled ship's sails. The patterning of floorcloths began simply as alternating checks which resembled tiles, sometimes with marbling. These tile patterns became more complicated and by the 19th century were usually stencilled.

The stencil patterns for home furnishings were usually made up of subjects which reflected the culture of the people producing them. For example, the tulip is known to be used traditionally by the Dutch and Germans and later became the symbol of the Pennsylvania Dutch. The heart motif is known to be of Scandinavian origin. Sometimes patterns reflected the recent history of the people. The bald eagle, the new national emblem of America in 1782, became a very popular motif for the colonists.

With the rise of the industrial revolution came the ability to reproduce pattern in great detail and quantity. Assembly line wallpapers and woven goods became available to the newly created middle classes at a relatively inexpensive price and the popularity of stencilling began to fade in the late 1800s.

For the first-time stenciller there are ready made stencils available from artist suppliers, craft shops, specialist decorative paint suppliers and even larger branches of DIY stores. These stencils are pre-cut and are ready to be applied. There are also many stencil pattern books available. These books do not usually have the stencil cut out, but they do have the advantage that you can enlarge or reduce the pattern with a photocopier and transfer the pattern to card or acetate. Either ready made or out of a book, this can be an easy way to persuade the wary painter to attempt stencilling.

If the ready made stencil isn't for you or you are ready to dig into the idea of designing your own, you can find inspiration from many sources. There are numerous books that provide

A highly stylized classical bathroom designed with columns, twining vines and a romantic balustrade, all available as commercial stencil patterns. This elegant room demonstrates just how effective stencil images can be to create a look that is totally individual and unique.

. . . .

the patterns and ornamental detail of periods in history. A very good source book is *The Grammar of Ornament*, by Owen Jones first published in 1857 and now available in reprint. You can use fabric and quilt patterns, china and tile patterns, rug patterns, wallpaper patterns, or illustrations from children's story·books as starting points for your stencil design.

The Gallery section of this book gives you some examples of stencil work by professionals. There is also a materials and basic techniques section which can be used as a reference to help you begin stencilling. It tells you what kind of material to make your stencil from, what kind of paint to use and how to apply it. The projects section gives you some ideas and hints about stencilling different types of surfaces and objects with step-by-step instructions to help guide you on your way to stencilling with confidence.

MATERIALS AND EQUIPMENT

ONE OF THE ADVANTAGES of stencilling is that you can begin with just a few simple tools. A brush, some paint and a stencil in any shape or form that you choose and away you go!

The following is a description of the basic pieces of equipment and some advice which may help you choose the right tools and materials for your stencilling projects.

STENCIL MATERIAL

Stencil card can be bought from artists' suppliers and craft stores. It is manila card that has been soaked in linseed oil. The linseed oil makes the card tough and pliable so that it can be bent around curved surfaces. The oiled card is somewhat waterproof, too. However, if you are using water-based paints and plan on using your stencil for lots of repeat patterning, you may want to give both sides a coat of spray paint to prevent the stencil from curling and becoming damaged.

If you are unable to obtain stencil card or you have become an avid stenciller and want to save the expense of buying stencil card, there are two methods for making your own. You will need thick cartridge paper or manila card, linseed oil or shellac, which is sometimes called knotting.

For the first method, brush both sides of the paper or card with linseed oil and leave to dry for a week. This very long drying time is the only disadvantage to the linseed oil method.

Remember the linseed oil makes the card or paper tough and pliable so that it can be bent around curved surfaces. If you are using this method you could do a few sheets at the same time so that when they are dry you will have a stock of oiled card which will last a while.

If you want to make stencil card quickly, you can try the second method. This uses shellac or knotting which usually dries within fifteen minutes. The method of application is the same as that of linseed oil, basically give both sides of the card or paper a coat and leave to dry. The shellac softens the card or paper and seals it, although not quite as well as the linseed oil method; however, it does have the advantage of being quick to employ.

The other material commonly used for stencils is **clear acetate**. Clear acetate has the advantage of being very easy to align for a stencil pattern with lots of repeats, such as wallpaper patterns or borders. It is also very easy to transfer your pattern to acetate because it is clear. You just lay the sheet of acetate over the top of your pattern and trace with a permanent marking pen. The major disadvantage of clear acetate is that it is quite slippery which makes it difficult to cut. It also has a tendency to split as you cut around corners or awkward angles.

Choose heavy grade acetate and take extra care when cutting. It might be worth considering restricting acetate to patterns which

are quite large and not very intricate, because the flimsiness of a cut acetate stencil can make it somewhat difficult to handle.

CUTTING TOOLS

The most tedious job in stencilling is cutting out the stencil. You can use a Stanley knife, a craft knife or a scalpel. The important thing is to have plenty of extra blades. As soon as a blade begins to show signs of being dull, it may not pierce the surface of the stencil card easily, so replace it. Your patience will not be tested and the stencil that you have spent so much time working on will not be ruined.

CUTTING SURFACE

You need to have a surface to cut your stencils which will protect your work surface. **Cutting mats** are made of a durable, 'self-healing' material that withstands repeated cutting. Their surface is non-skid which keeps things from slipping around too much. They make the tedious job of stencil cutting much easier. They are expensive but are a good investment once you become an avid stenciller.

Hardboard is an inexpensive and good alternative to a cutting mat. It does, however, dull the blades of your cutting knife more quickly than a cutting mat.

It is not recommended that you use a surface such as chip board or particle board or even a plank of wood to cut your stencils on. These surfaces have a texture or grain which will tend to hold or guide the tip of your cutting blade and you may find that you are struggling to guide the blade around your pattern.

Another excellent alternative on which to cut stencils is an old **telephone book**. It is firm enough to allow you to apply pressure when cutting and the surface will not blunt the blade very quickly. When the pages that you have been cutting on have become shredded, you just tear them away and start again with fresh pages. Telephone books can be difficult when cutting large stencils but are fine for small patterns and they are terrific for beginners who don't want to invest much money at the early stages.

PAINT

Choosing the type of paint to use for stencilling can often seem confusing. Here we will try to answer some of the questions which arise when choosing paint.

Most stencilling should be done with paint which dries quickly. This allows you to lift your stencil and reposition it for continued stencilling. Water-based paints such as **emulsions** (latexes) dry quickly, come in many colours, and can be cleaned up with just hot, soapy water. Generally, they should be applied over surfaces which are the same base, i.e. emulsion should be applied over emulsion as this will not adhere to surfaces painted with certain oil-based paints, such as gloss. However, acrylics (water-based) over an eggshell (oil-based) background are frequently employed successfully but must be protected with polyurethane varnish.

You may want to use a slow drying **oil-based paint** for stencilling when you work on a very glossy surface. This does have one advantage in that you can blend the colour subtly because the paint is slow drying.

You must be careful when lifting the stencil not to smudge the paint, and it is very difficult to stencil in oils a pattern which has lots of repeats or points which need to connect because you cannot lay the stencil over what you have just stencilled until it is dry. Oil-based paints and brushes must be cleaned with white spirit.

Spray paints are tough and are formulated to adhere to many difficult surfaces, wood, metal, fabric, glass or ceramics, (although there are specific paints available for some of these materials). They have the added advantage of drying very quickly. The disadvantage of using spray paint is that it may not come in the exact colour that you might choose for your stencil work. The key to mixing colour when spray painting is to apply different colour sprays and to apply the spray by lightly misting rather than giving the spray one long blast. You can use this light misting to blend very different colours to create a colour which is close to the one you want and which has subtle shading. Also, the stencilling will have a soft texture all its own.

Artists' acrylics which can be found in art suppliers and crafts stores comes in a large range of colours and are excellent for stencilling. They dry quickly and when dry are waterproof and hard. They have a relatively thick consistency and are less likely to bleed under the stencil. The one disadvantage of artists' acrylics is that they come in small tubes and if used on a large stencilling project can become expensive. However, because they are water-based they can be used to tint emulsions.

PAINT APPLICATORS

The most common tool used to apply paint through the stencil is the **stencil brush**, which is available from artist suppliers and craft stores and some specialist decorating supply centres.

Stencil brushes have a round ferrule, densely packed with short, stiff bristles. These types of brush do not carry any quantity of paint, therefore preventing paint from bleeding under the edge of the stencil.

If you are just beginning to stencil there is no need to invest in stencil brushes. You can use a small, 2.5 cm (1 in) decorating brush instead. Just be sure that the bristles are stiff. You can go one step better than this by taking an old decorating brush and cutting the bristles down so that they are about 1-2.5 cm (½-1 in) long. If you do this you may find that you never need to buy a stencil brush.

Pieces of upholstery **foam rubber** can also be used as paint applicators. You should cut the foam to 2.5-5 cm (1-2 in) square and about 5 cm (2 in) thick. You can use smaller pieces of foam for stencilling tiny spaces. Foam is inexpensive – you may even have an old cushion around the house waiting to be cut up - and you can just throw your squares away when you are done. Stencilling with foam rubber tends to be a bit messier than stencilling with a brush because you have no handle between your hand and the paint but this is not a problem if you are using water-based paints which clean easily.

An alternative to foam rubber is a **natural sponge**. Although more expensive, this gives a wonderful soft touch when applying the paint.

SPRAY PAINTS

RED

JADE

FABRIC PAINTS

CERAMIC PAINT

SCALPEL

CUTTING MAT

TAPE MEASURE

STEEL RULER

SANDPAPER

CARTRIDGE PAPER

EMERY PAPER

FOAM RUBBER

ARTISTS' ACRYLICS

PERMANENT MARKER

NEWSPAPER

PENCIL

CLEAR ACETATE

STENCIL BRUSHES

GRAPH PAPER

WHITE ERASER

TRACING PAPER

CARBON PAPER

STENCIL CARD

MASKING TAPE

SCISSORS

BASIC TECHNIQUES

IF YOU ARE CREATING your own design, don't be afraid to sketch and experiment. Work in pencil so that you can erase and change elements of your design until you have a pattern that you are pleased with. If you are new to stencilling, it is best to start with simple designs and work your way up to more complicated patterns.

DRAWING A DESIGN

Take ideas for patterns from books, magazines, wallpaper and textile designs. If you are decorating a children's room, explore children's books – always well illustrated and with plenty of simple, bold shapes which can make ideal templates for a stencil. When you have found something you like, see how well it will convert to a stencil. It is best to choose a simple shape, or else to simplify the object you have chosen. Photocopy or trace the piece, then look at it in terms of simple lines and shapes.

When you have a design that you are pleased with, fill it in with a felt tip marker so that you can begin to see what the image will look like as a stencil.

You must remember to include 'bridges' as an integral part of your design. They are a necessary element of a stencil because they hold it together. They should occur at regular intervals and their frequency should become part of the rhythm of the pattern. Bridges should also be designed in the same feeling as the rest of the stencil. Large and bold, slashing diagonals, delicate and sweeping – their size and weight depends on the size of the stencil. But don't make them too small or they may not hold the stencil together when you begin to paint.

If you find a design in a book or magazine that you would like to convert into a stencil, but discover that is too small, use a photocopier to enlarge the design. If you do not have access to a photocopier, you can scale the design up by drawing a square grid over it. Number and letter the vertical and horizontal lines. Then decide the size you would like the final design to be. Draw a corresponding larger grid on a piece of drawing or tracing paper. Now carefully draw the design on the new grid, using the lines as your guide. Remember to include bridges in the pattern and any registration marks or centre lines which will help you align the stencil later. You can use graph paper to help save you time drawing grids.

If you are taking a pattern from a piece of fabric, photocopy it first then draw a grid on to the photocopy.

TRANSFERRING THE DESIGN TO CARD

If you are using stencil card, it is quite straightforward to use carbon paper to transfer your design. Just place the carbon paper between the image and the stencil card, tape it in place with masking tape and trace over the design firmly with a ballpoint pen. Be sure to peel back a corner of the carbon and take a peek when you think that you have finished to be sure that you have traced everything.

You can also use display-grade spray adhesive to permanently glue photocopies to oiled stencil

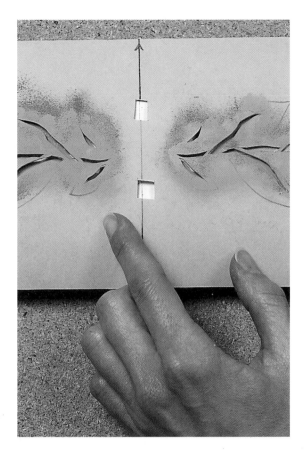

Draw a vertical centre line on the stencil card and cut out tiny registration windows. These will help you align the stencil when you are ready to position it.

. . . .

card. This grade of spray adhesive is waterproof so that it will not react with water-based paints when you are stencilling. Spray the back of your photocopy and spray the surface of your card; wait until they become tacky and then carefully position the photocopy on to the card. Use a decorating brush, wallpaper seam roller or even your hand to smooth the surface and remove any bubbles.

You can also transfer your design to stencil card by first drawing it in very soft pencil on tracing paper. Turn the tracing paper over and tape it to the stencil card so that it does not shift. Then trace the now reversed image of your drawing, pressing down firmly. The image will be transferred from the pencil image on the underside of the tracing.

If your design is bigger then a single piece of stencil card, you can join two pieces of card together making a piece large enough to incorporate your whole design. To do this you must butt two edges of stencil card up against one another and use waterproof masking tape along the seam on both sides. Then draw your pattern as usual.

It is probably easiest to transfer your design to clear acetate. Just place the acetate over the design, tape it into place so that it does not move, and trace with a permanent marking pen.

Once your design has been transferred it is a good idea to ink it in with a marker or coloured pencil to help you see it as a solid pattern and to be certain of the shapes that you are going to cut away. It is very important to remember to include bridges to help hold your stencil and image together.

Simple designs can be drawn directly on to the stencil card using a felt tip pen, although it is probably best to experiment with pencil and paper first to make sure you are happy with the motif you have created.

. . . .

When cutting out small, intricate shapes, turn the stencil around as you work. Always cut on a suitable surface such as a 'self-healing' cutting mat. Use a sharp blade in your scalpel and replace it as soon as it shows signs of becoming blunt.

. . . .

CUTTING THE STENCIL

Always cut on a suitable surface: a cutting mat (available from art and graphics suppliers) or a thick piece of cardboard are ideal. Begin cutting small shapes before large ones. If you cut large ones first, you will weaken your stencil material and it later becomes difficult to cut out the smaller shapes.

Work from the centre of your pattern outwards so that you run your hand across the surface of the stencil as little as possible to avoid any damage. Use a scalpel or very sharp craft knife, drawing the blade toward yourself and turning the stencil as you go so that the blade is always being drawn towards you. Try to keep the action of moving the blade as smooth and fluid as possible.

If you make a mistake, you can repair it by applying masking tape to both sides of the card. If the masking tape is covering any cut-out areas, use the knife to cut out the shape again, carefully slicing through the masking tape.

SURFACE PREPARATION

Any surface to be stencilled (or indeed painted in any way) should be clean and free from any loose or flaky material. Walls, furniture and accessories should be cleaned thoroughly with hot, soapy water and rinsed well. (Use sugar soap to remove grease and grime and to give you a really clean surface.)

If you are working on a piece which has never been painted before and you plan to use a base coat, you need to use a primer or undercoat suitable for that type of material. There are different types of primers for wood and metal.

cottons, linens, and silks should be pre-washed to remove any sizing and to shrink them. Natural fibres hold colour well and you may find that they are the best to stencil. Once the piece has been stencilled it is advisable not to wash it too frequently.

Some surfaces will need to be primed first. Sailcloth or canvas, for example, must be primed to shrink the cloth and enable you to apply a basecoat. If you intend to apply a background colour to bare wood, you will also need to prime it first.

. . . .

The surface can then be painted in your chosen base colour.

Wooden and concrete floors can both be stencilled successfully. They should be washed with a degreaser and rinsed until the water runs clean. Wooden floors should be sanded until they are smooth. However, it is not necessary to strip the varnish off floors before stencilling. Oil-based paints and car spray paint will adhere to varnish, but you must protect your stencilling with three coats of polyurethane varnish when you have finished.

Look at the surface that you are about to stencil. Are there any elements such as hinges or knobs which can easily be removed so that they do not get in the way of the stencil? If they can't be removed, you may have to cut notches in the stencil to fit round them.

Items made of fabric, such as window blinds, tablecloths and cushion covers should be cut to size before stencilling. Natural fibres such as

Before you position the stencil, you should draw guide lines on the surface to be decorated, so that the pattern can be placed accurately. This is especially important on large surfaces, such as walls or floors, and items which require precise alignment, such as a dado rail or skirting board.

. . . .

POSITIONING THE STENCIL

You must take the time to make accurate registration marks or guide lines for your stencilling. In repeat patterns such as borders you need to mark the position of each image. If you skip this step you may regret it by ending up with a pattern which is slightly crooked or which is badly out of alignment when it meets.

It may be necessary for you to find the centre point on a square or rectangular surface. To do this, you need to draw in the diagonals with a ruler or straight edge. The centre is the point where they cross. To find the centre on large surfaces such as walls or floors you can use lengths of string tacked to corners and run diagonally across the surface. Again, your centre point is where they cross.

You must use a spirit level for accurate horizontal alignment and a plumb line to give

There are various methods of stencilling: both how you apply the paint or colour and the type of stencil material that you use.

Top: A paper doiley is used as a stencil, so no drawing or cutting is required. In this case, car spray paint is used to create a lacy effect on a piece of plain fabric.

Bottom left: Artists' acrylics are employed to brighten up a terracotta flowerpot. The paint is applied with a small scrap of foam rubber. Use a fresh piece for each colour.

Bottom right: A base coat of eggshell has been applied to a tin tray. The paint - in this instance, artists' acrylic - is dabbed on to the surface with a stencil brush through a clear acetate stencil.

. . . .

or straight. Do all your marking lightly in pencil or in chalk. Any pencil that remains after you have finished stencilling can be erased with a

Tape the stencil into place with low-tack masking tape. This will prevent the stencil moving while you are applying the paint. The stencil can be removed easily afterwards, and should cause no damage to the item being decorated.

. . . .

you a true vertical. Do not rely on the horizontal or vertical elements of the room, such as door or window casings, to be perfectly level

white eraser which will not leave any marks on the surface. (Pink erasers, like the ones found on the end of pencils, do leave smudge marks and should never be used in any decorative painting.)

Once you have made guide marks on the surface, you can position the stencil and hold it firmly in place with low tack masking tape, pins or thumb tacks – all of which allow you to lift off the stencil easily for repositioning.

You can also use mounting-grade spray adhesive to hold the stencil in place. This grade of spray adhesive is not permanent and allows you to lift off the stencil and reposition it a few times before the stencil needs re-coating. To coat the stencil with spray adhesive, place the stencil right side down on protective paper and

Spray adhesive is a good option for holding intricate stencils, such as pieces of lace or paper doilies, into place. The adhesive covers the whole stencil and ensures that the paint cannot seep under any of the pattern. The stencil can be lifted off easily once the paint has been applied.

. . . .

coat with a thin mist of adhesive. Wait a minute or two to allow the adhesive to become tacky before positioning it, adhesive side down, on the surface. If you need to use the wrong side of the stencil, ie, if you are turning the design over to obtain a mirror image, you can dust the tacky side with talcum powder before continuing. This method of holding the stencil in position works exceptionally well when you are working on a slippery, shiny surface, such as glass or ceramic tiles. It also helps give you a very clean outline with very little bleed.

APPLICATION OF PAINT

Emulsion, acrylic and oil paint can be applied through the stencil with a small decorating brush, stencilling brush, a piece of foam rubber or a natural sponge.

The trick in stencilling is to apply the paint as 'dryly' as possible. It can help to pour some of the paint on to some sort of a palette – an old saucer or the lid of a paint can will do. Dip just the end of the stencil brush into the paint and dab off the excess on to scrap or kitchen paper. Then use a quick pouncing or stippling motion to apply the paint. Try not to scrub or brush the paint through the stencil as this may cause the paint to seep under the edge. When you are using a pattern that is going to be built up in a few colours, stencil all of one colour first before moving on to the next.

Spray paint should be applied with a gentle pumping action that will produce a mist. Hold the can at the manufacturer's recommended distance from the surface or a little closer for smaller detail and at a slight angle to the surface to be sprayed. Gently pump the nozzle while slightly moving the can. Spray the stencil all over in this way to build up a thin even layer of colour and then spray again to build up more colour. The idea is to build up soft layers of mist. You can work in either the same colour or in different colours if you have chosen to combine different colour sprays. A spray painted stencil built up in this way will produce soft and subtle shading.

One thing that you must remember when spray painting is to mask off areas that you do not want sprayed. No matter how controlled you are, the 'overspray' can creep into unwanted places. You will also be left with lines where the edge of the stencil card or acetate was placed, which will look particularly unattractive.

As a general rule, you should build up colours from the lightest shade to the darkest, whether you are using liquid paint or spray paint. Darker shades naturally cover or lay over lighter shades. The colour also seems to be truer than painting light over dark. Light colours and shades can appear muddied if applied over darker ones. If you must paint a light shade over a

One of the joys of stencilling is the subtle shading and merging of colours that can be achieved, regardless of the type of paint used. Here, artists' acrylics are dabbed through the stencil with a natural sponge. The sponge gives a lovely soft edge to the colours; work quickly, one after the other.

. . . .

darker one, you may find that you need to make the light colour even lighter to compensate for it covering a darker one.

FINISHING AND PROTECTING

On some surfaces, such as ceramics, tiles and glass, mistakes can be quickly remedied because the paint is easily removed. For other surfaces, it is unlikely that you will be able to erase or dramatically alter the motif once it has been applied. However, you can make amendments, after the stencil card or acetate has been removed, by using a fine paintbrush. This is simple enough to do, especially if the stencil has

smudged or bled. However, as many stencil designs have a rather naive appeal, a little softness and blurring will not matter.

When your pattern is completely dry it is worth protecting it with a coat of either polyurethane or acrylic varnish. This is especially important with water-based paints, or stencils applied to furniture or floors.

CARE OF STENCILS

Stencils may become clogged up with paint. You can clean them up by carefully slicing the built up layers of paint away from the cut away areas with a craft knife. Or you may choose to make a fresh stencil.

Before you store stencils, you should let them dry out completely. Acetate stencils that have been painted with water-based paints can be carefully wiped clean with a damp cloth. Label your stencil patterns and store them flat with sheets of paper or card between them.

GALLERY

OVER THE NEXT FEW pages we explore the ways in which stencilled designs have been used on walls, floors, windows, cupboards, ceramics and screens, among others, to transform these humdrum household items into eye-catching pieces of furniture or spectacular room settings.

All the stencils featured are the works of professional artists and designers, and many of the stencils are available commercially by mail order or through retail outlets. However, it is hoped you will find inspiration and encouragement from these works to design and create your own patterns and images which will give your home a touch of individuality.

~

**French Wine
Country**
THE STENCIL STORE
A burgeoning vine trails
down the sides of a
Gothic-style window.
The stencil was applied
with fast drying, hard
stencil paint.

Pineapple Firescreen

ELEANOR ALLITT

This stylized pineapple motif has been sprayed on to a plain wooden firescreen using car spray paint. The sides of the panel have been stencilled with a simple panel which reflects the main design.

. . . .

Garden Room

PAVILION

Two wall panels depicting fruits of the orchard sit above a classic balustrade. Stencilled on to a colourwashed wall, these designs offset a conservatory style room.

. . . .

Trailing Ivy

THE STENCIL STORE
Trailing vines or
creeping plants are
popular stencil motifs
for walls and doorways.
This pattern has been
used in a free and artistic
way to emphasise the
attractive sloping
ceiling.

. . . .

Farmstead Bucket

KATHY FILLION RITCHIE
An old-fashioned pail
has been given a new
lease of life with a coat
of paint and a simple,
rustic motif stencilled
on to its side.

. . . .

Decorated ceramics
LYN LE GRICE
Bowls and cups have
been decorated with
different stencil motifs
in earthy hues to create
a coordinated look.
. . . .

Floral Hatbox
ELEANOR ALLITT
Three individual stencil
designs have been
incorporated on to this
marblized hatbox. The
sides feature a rose and
doiley pattern, the top
of the lid shows an
arrangement of
carnations, while a leaf
motif circles the side of
the lid.
. . . .

Wild Animal Chest

THE STENCIL STORE

An unusual and exciting effect has been created on this plain chest of drawers. The lilac paint appears to peel away to reveal a group of stencilled animals marching off the chest and into the bedroom.
. . . .

Painted Rug

THE STENCIL STORE
A good example of the
effectiveness of
stencilling directly on to
plain wood. This
stencilled rug appears to
be a natural
floorcovering.
. . . .

Rose and Peony Urn

THE STENCIL STORE
A traditional and
classical style stencil.
Roses, peonies and ivy
spill out of this urn.

. . . .

Corner Cabinet

LYN LE GRICE
Rural topics are popular
stencil images. Sheep in
the lee of an oak tree
decorate the front of
this cupboard in this
intricate stencil.

. . . .

Anatolian Design

STEWART WALTON

Rich earthy colours are used on these hessian cushions to evoke the look of an ancient exotic weave. Artists' acrylics were applied through various stencils with a stencil brush.

. . . .

Wallflower Screen

ELEANOR ALLITT

A three-panelled pine screen has been stencilled with a wallflower-inspired design. Each panel has been stencilled in a slightly different way, giving a touch of variety and interest to the whole design.

. . . .

Bathroom Cabinet

THE STENCIL STORE

The glass panels in this attractive bathroom cabinet have been stencilled using a fast-drying hard stencil paint. Stencilled shells form a border around the rest of the room.

. . . .

WALL CABINET

KATHY FILLION RITCHIE

STENCILS CAN BE USED to accent unusual shapes found in furniture and in architecture which might otherwise go unnoticed. This small, sage green cupboard has a 'tombstone'-shaped door. A floral patterned stencil was designed to emphasise the semi-circular shape at the top of the door and a corner detail was used to complete the effect.

The stencilling was achieved using four separate stencils, two stencils for the flower details within the arch and in the corners, and two stencils for the leaf detail which followed.

~

MATERIALS AND EQUIPMENT

• *tracing paper* • *pencil* • *stencil card* • *masking tape* • *ruler* • *scalpel* • *artists' acrylics in burnt sienna, raw umber, chrome oxide green, white and cream* • *small pieces of foam rubber* • *palette or saucers* • *scrap paper for blotting*

. . . . . .

1 Transfer the patterns on page 90 to stencil card, using one of the methods described on pages 14–15. Cut out the stencil with a scalpel. Measure the centre of the arch on the door and make a pencil mark. Position the arched flower stencil on the door, aligning the centre of the stencil with the mark on the door. Hold the stencil in place with pieces of masking tape.

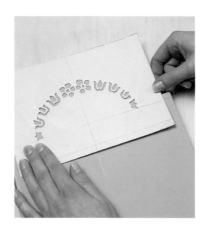

2 Dip a small piece of foam rubber into the burnt sienna base colour and blot off the excess on some scrap paper. Apply the paint in small dabbing motions, being careful not to scrub or drag the sponge, which may cause the paint to bleed under the edge of the stencil.

3 Mix a little cream colour with the burnt sienna base colour. Dip a fresh piece of foam into the cream mixture, blot off the excess and very lightly sponge a highlight which breaks up the surface of the flowers and gives them texture. Remove the stencil and leave to dry.

4 Position the corner flower stencil and tape it into position. Paint as in steps 2 and 3. Wipe the surface of the stencil, turn it over and position it in the opposite corner of the cabinet door and paint as before.

5 Once the arched flower pattern has dried, position the arched leaf pattern, lining up the flowers underneath with the little registration window which has been cut out on the leaf stencil. Tape the stencil into place with masking tape.

6 Apply paint using pieces of foam. The leaf colour is built up from chrome oxide green with white and a touch of raw umber. With the top stencil complete, you can now add the leaf detail to the corner motifs, using the leaf colours you have just mixed and following step 4 as your guide.

SILK SCARF

MELANIE WILLIAMS

BECAUSE OF ITS LIGHT and delicate qualities, silk is an ideal fabric to decorate with paint techniques. Here, the scarf has first been painted with a mixture of pale colour washes to provide a perfect background for the stencilled spiral shapes, which are applied later when the silk has dried.

~

MATERIALS AND EQUIPMENT

- silk • fabric paints
- tracing paper • pencil
- scalpel • stencil card
- masking tape • tape measure • pins • scissors
- palette or small saucers
- soft paintbrush
- iron • small natural sponge
- coloured sewing thread

. . . . . .

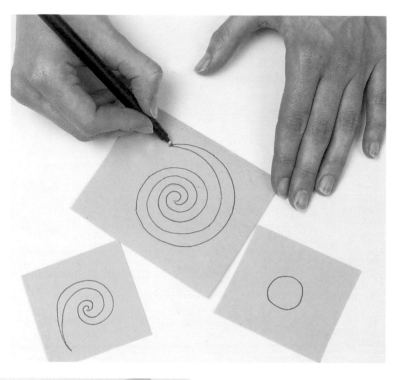

1 Using the patterns on page 90, transfer the swirls and dot on to the stencil card.

2 Cut out the stencil patterns using a sharp scalpel or craft knife and a cutting mat or piece of hardboard.

3 Using a tape measure and pins as a guide, cut the silk to approximately 94 cm (37 in) square with sharp scissors.

4 Dip the silk into cold water to wet it thoroughly, then gently wring out.

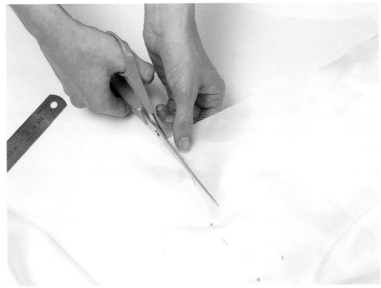

5 Choose the colours for the background and place a little of each into a palette or small saucer. Apply the paints in turn to the wet silk with a soft paintbrush, allowing the colours to merge and bleed. Press the silk with a warm iron before it dries.

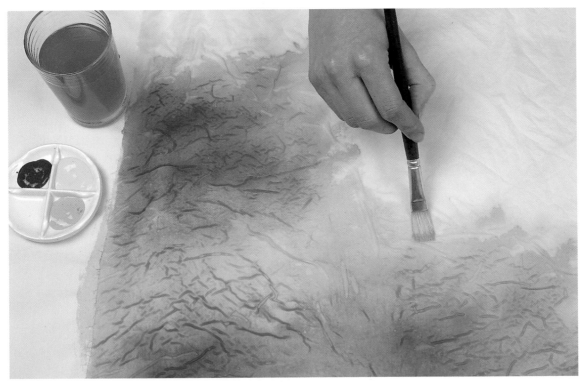

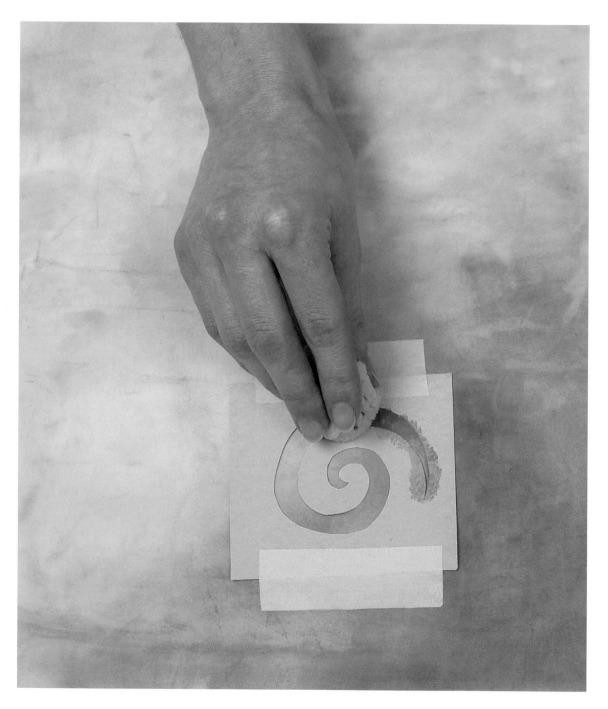

6 When the silk is completely dry, stick the stencil into place using the masking tape. Apply the paint to the stencil with the sponge, dabbing the colour on in quick movements. Lift the stencil card and repeat elsewhere, to create a random pattern. Press the silk with a warm iron on the wrong side.

7 Once all the swirls have been stencilled, add the dots in contrasting colours. Press again with a warm iron on the wrong side of the fabric.

8 Press a small hem all round the silk and sew a neat running or hemming stitch to complete the scarf.

PERSONAL STATIONERY

MELANIE WILLIAMS

THIS CRISP, STYLISH writing paper and coordinating envelopes can be produced so easily and inexpensively, yet it is sure to impress and delight anyone who receives it.

It is created by sponging acrylics or poster paints through the stencils on to quality, textured paper. The instructions show you how to make matching envelopes, as well as the writing paper itself. Templates are provided on page 91 to help you.

~

MATERIALS AND EQUIPMENT

• good quality paper in pale colour • paper glue or spray adhesive • tracing paper • pencil • scalpel • steel ruler • masking tape • stencil card • acrylic or poster paints • natural sponge • palette or saucers

. . . . . .

1 Using a pencil, lightly mark out the finished size for the writing paper – 28 x 21 cm (11 x 8 ¼ in) is a convenient size. Mark out at least six pieces. For the envelopes, enlarge the pattern on page 91 and transfer it to the good quality writing paper. Cut out all the pieces using a scalpel with a steel ruler on a cutting mat. Use the back of a scissor blade to score down the fold lines on the envelopes where indicated on the pattern. Apply adhesive to the envelope, following the pattern, and stick down.

2 Once the writing paper and envelopes have been prepared, trace the stencil motifs on page 91 and transfer them on to the stencil card. Cut out the stencils using the scalpel.

3 Tape the bird stencil to the middle of the top of the paper and sponge on two or three colours of your choice. Let the colours merge slightly for a more natural effect. Leave the motif to dry, then remove the stencil.

4 Tape the branch stencil to each side of the bird. Sponge on more colour – a realistic mixture of greens, for example. Finally, tape the flower stencil on top of the branch and sponge on a bright, contrasting colour. Repeat this technique for each of the papers and then again for the envelopes.

TIN TRAY

CHRIS FOX

OLD TINWARE presents endless opportunities for stencilling projects. You can transform used watering cans, cake tins, old biscuit barrels, baking trays, tin cans or cash boxes.

This tray has been painted in pale yellow eggshell and stencilled with deep rose pink acrylic paint – 'afternoon tea' colours that will set off prettily patterned china. After stencilling, a crackle glaze was applied to give an antique effect and the tray was finished with a coat of polyurethane varnish.

Used tinware showing signs of rust should be rubbed down with wire wool and treated with a rust remover before being primed with a metal primer.

~

1 Coat the tray with pale yellow eggshell. Allow to dry then mark off the centre point of each side of the tray. Transfer the motif from page 91 on to the clear acetate, enlarging or reducing it to fit your tray (make sure that the motif does not extend beyond any of the centre marks you have made). Cut out the stencil and lay it face down on scrap paper. Spray with adhesive and allow to dry for a few seconds.

2 Place the stencil neatly into one corner of the tray and press it down firmly – use a wallpaper seam roller to help you – so that no paint can seep underneath.

3 Mix the acrylic paint with a little water until it is creamy. Dip the stencil brush into the paint and dab off any excess on to some kitchen paper. Apply the paint to the tray through the stencil, using a light circular movement. A slight variation in pressure will create an attractive dappled effect. Allow to dry for a few seconds.

4 Gently peel off the stencil and repeat the process in the corner diagonally opposite. Apply the paint, peel off the stencil and wipe clean before flipping it over and using in the other two corners. When all the corners are complete, allow to dry thoroughly before applying a coat of polyurethane varnish. If you would like an antique, crazed effect, use a crackle glaze kit – available from craft shops – and follow the manufacturer's instructions.

TERRACOTTA POTS

KATHY FILLION RITCHIE

STENCILLING BOLD, BRIGHT colours on to little terracotta flowerpots has given them a Mediterranean or even Mexican look. These little pots can be used for small plants, as candle holders or simply as small tidies for odd household bits.

As the design has a naive quality, you do not need to be too exact when lining up the stencils. In some instances, holding the stencils by hand while you apply the paint will be all that is required.

~

MATERIALS AND EQUIPMENT

• terracotta flowerpots • artists'
acrylics in white, light chrome
yellow, ultramarine blue and
paynes grey • tracing paper
• pencil • stencil card • scalpel
• pieces of foam rubber
• masking tape

......

1 Transfer the patterns on page
91 on to stencil card and cut
out in the usual way. Position the
first stencil in place around the
body of the pot and tape into
place. Apply the paint using a
piece of foam rubber for each
colour and alternating the colours
in each shape. Here, we have
used artists' acrylics in light
chrome yellow and ultramarine
blue mixed with white.

2 Position the circle stencil on
the rim of the pot and hold it
in position or tape it if you prefer
while you stencil. Work your
way around the rim, alternating
the colours.

3 When the paint is dry, position the outline stencil in place over the coloured shapes. The outline stencil doesn't have to be positioned perfectly over the shapes. This design is supposed to have a hand printed or stamped appearance. Use paynes grey artists' acrylic as the outline colour.

4 Position the circle outline over one of the circles and hold or tape into place. Paint as in step 3, working your way around the rim until all the circles are outlined.

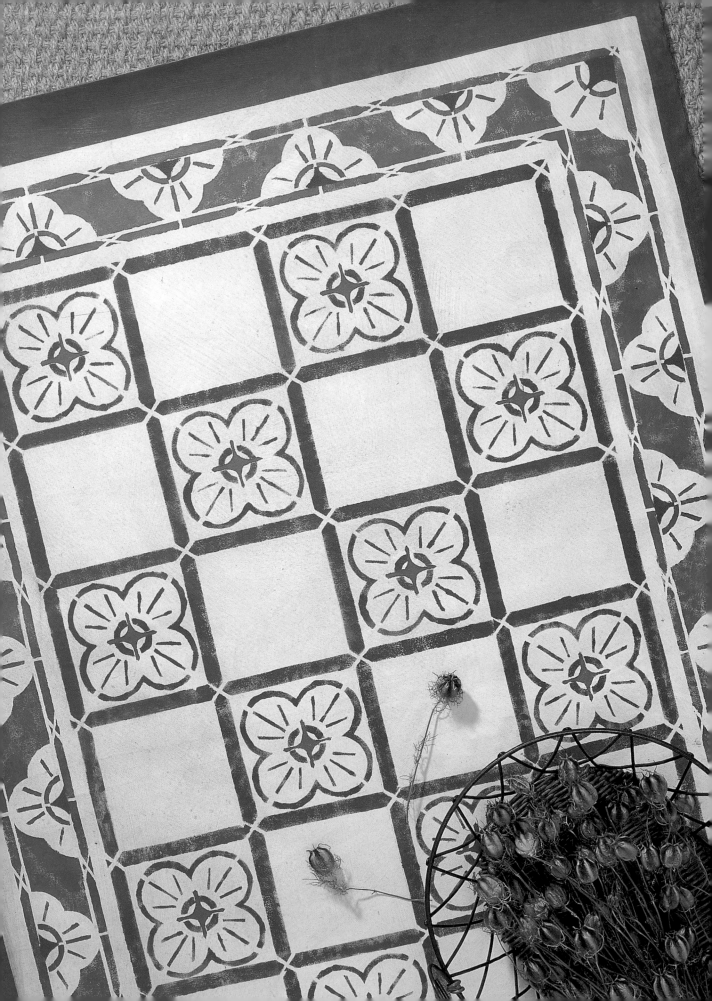

FLOORCLOTH

KATHY FILLION RITCHIE

THIS WONDERFUL floor covering is perhaps one of the more challenging projects in the book, but one that is immensely satisfying to undertake.

Heavy canvas is primed and painted before an intricate pattern is stencilled on using three basic colours. Once complete, the floorcloth is given several coats of varnish to protect the prized design from wearing away under the daily toil of many feet.

You can, of course, adapt the design for a tablecloth or bed throw, using a lighterweight fabric and omitting the varnish at the end.

~

MATERIALS AND EQUIPMENT

• *piece of heavy artists' canvas or sailcloth* • *1 litre (2 pt) acrylic primer* • *artists' acrylics in white, yellow ochre, burnt sienna, deep cadmium red, hooker's green, raw umber* • *PVA glue* • *acrylic or polyurethane varnish* • *2.5 cm (1 in) masking tape* • *tracing paper* • *staplegun (with 5 mm/¼ in staples) or thumb tacks* • *large decorating brush or roller* • *soft natural-bristled decorating brush 5-7.5 cm (2-3 in) wide* • *sandpaper* • *pencil* • *clear acetate* • *stencil card* • *pieces of foam rubber* • *scalpel*
. . . . . .

1 Probably the most difficult element of this project is finding a wooden surface such as a table or floor where you can attach your canvas so it will be undisturbed for the priming stage (step 2). The entire piece of canvas must be primed at the same time because this causes it to shrink. This shrinking only happens once, so if you have to remove the staples or tacks after the primer has dried, it will not matter. Staple or tack the cloth to a wooden surface stretching it smooth. Staples or tacks should be placed roughly 7-10 cm (3-4 in) apart.

2 Paint the cloth with acrylic primer using a wide decorating brush or a roller. Let this dry completely. Allow roughly two hours. Sand lightly with fine sandpaper. If you would like to fill more of the weave of the fabric, you can give the cloth another coat of primer. Allow to dry and sand again. You can now remove the tacks or staples, because the weave of the fabric has been filled and it will have shrunk.

3 Mix a yellow ochre and white acrylic to a soft yellow. Add water to this to create a thin transparent wash. Apply this wash to the canvas using a soft, natural-bristled decorating brush. When dry, mark a centre line on the cloth.

4 Transfer the larger patterns on page 92 on to clear acetate and cut out in the usual way. Begin stencilling with the inner pattern and work your way to the outer pattern and border. Position the stencil on one side of the centre line and tape into place. Remember to begin far enough in from the outside edge to allow for the border pattern and the solid painted border.

5 Mix burnt sienna, deep cadmium red and white artists' acrylic to a soft terracotta colour. Apply the paint using a piece of foam rubber. Remember to remove the excess paint from the foam so that you can work as 'dryly' as possible.

57
· · · ·

6 This pattern builds up by alternating the patterned and the empty squares, always working from the centre line. The pattern doesn't need to be totally 'blocked' in with paint. It is better to allow the pattern to be slightly broken.

7 The border stencil has been designed to begin at a corner. This stencil is best made from clear acetate so that it is easy to align with the centre squares. Tape it into place. Mix hooker's green, yellow ochre and white artists' acrylics to produce this green. Apply the paint through the stencil using foam rubber and work as dryly as possible.

8 Reposition the border stencil and tape into place. You may want to use masking tape to cover the corner part of the pattern so that you do not accidentally sponge over it when you are in a position away from the corner. But you will have to take this tape off when you get to a corner. Work your way around the entire cloth until you have completed the border pattern.

9 Now with the basic pattern complete, add the central motifs to the border pattern and the inner grid pattern. Transfer the motifs on to stencil card which is easier to manipulate. Use the terracotta colour of the inner grid pattern over the green border pattern.

10 To paint the crosses on the inner terracotta pattern, position the stencil and apply the green border colour. These are very small stencils that are quick to apply so there is no need to tape them into place. Just hold the stencils in position with your fingers while you stencil.

11 Use 2.5 cm (1 in) wide masking tape to block off a band around the border pattern. Be sure to use a craft knife or scalpel to create sharp, square corners for the outside band.

12 Use the soft decorating brush to apply a terracotta band to the outside edge. When the paint is dry, remove the tape. Now apply a coat of acrylic or polyurethane varnish. Allow to dry completely.

13 If you haven't already pulled out the staples or tacks, do so now and turn the canvas over. Turn back a 4–5 cm (1 ½ –2 in) hem and mitre the corners. Use undiluted PVA glue to stick the hem down, applying the glue liberally. Now give the floorcloth two more coats of varnish on the right side, sanding lightly between each coat. Then give the back of the cloth a coat of varnish or diluted PVA glue to protect it.

CHINTZ CUSHION

CHRIS FOX

STENCILLING ON TO FABRIC allows you to design your own textiles and opens up endless possibilities for creating an individual look on both soft furnishings and clothes.

This chintz-style cushion cover has been created by stencilling through a paper doiley with spray paint. A cut-out floral motif from another piece of fabric has been bonded to the centre of the lace stencil for added interest. Choose natural fabrics like linen, cotton or calico, but test the paint on a scrap first, as absorbency can vary and you may need to apply two or three coats to achieve the colour required.

Once stencilled, the fabric can be made up into a cushion cover in the usual way.

MATERIALS AND EQUIPMENT

- *square of fabric* • *paper doiley* • *spray paint* • *spray adhesive* • *masking tape*
- *wallpaper seam roller*
- *scrap paper*

......

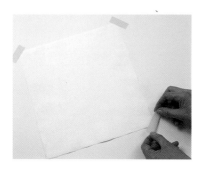

1 Lay the fabric right side up on to a large sheet of scrap paper. Make sure the paper will protect all the surrounding surfaces from the spray paint mist which will inevitably ensue once you begin. Fix the fabric down at each corner with masking tape.

2 Place the doiley face down on a sheet of scrap paper and spray with a light coating of adhesive. Allow it to dry for a few seconds.

3 Turn the doiley over and position it in the centre of the fabric and press down firmly so that no paint will be able to seep underneath. For the best results, use a wallpaper seam roller and apply firm pressure all over.

4 Spray paint over the cloth, ensuring it covers the doiley and right up to all edges of the fabric. Hold the can about 15 cm (6 in) from the surface and use a gentle pumping action on the button. Move the can slightly and smoothly from side to side to prevent build up in any one area.

5 Leave to dry for a few seconds before gently peeling off the doiley. As a finishing touch you can apply a circle of contrasting fabric to the centre of the lacy design using fabric glue or an iron-on bonding web.

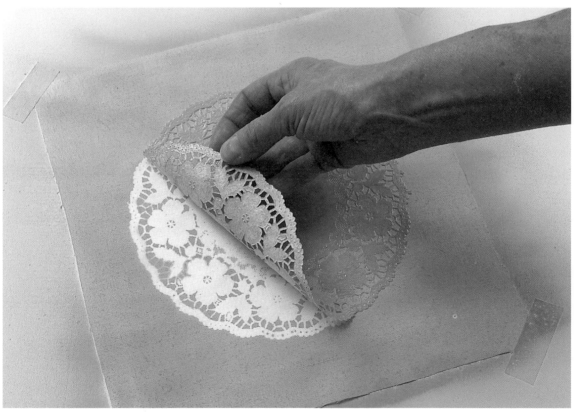

SMALL CHEST OF DRAWERS

KATHY FILLION RITCHIE

A LOVELY JEWELLERY cache or herb and spice store, this little chest of drawers has been given a decorative flourish with a simple floral stencil applied in a light cream colour on blue. Pick up a similar chest in gift, stationery or department stores and decorate in the colours of your choice. The handles were removed to make the stencilling easier.

~

MATERIALS AND EQUIPMENT

● *tracing paper* ● *artists'
acrylics in white and yellow
ochre or cream coloured
emulsion* ● *pencil* ● *stencil
card* ● *scalpel* ● *pieces of
foam rubber* ● *masking tape*
● *ruler* ● *palette or saucers*
● *sandpaper*
. . . . . .

1 This stencil is cut with a 1 cm (½ in) border which positions it perfectly in the corners of the front of the chest, so there is no measuring or marking to do. The border line is cut long enough so that it overlaps itself when the stencil is repositioned. The basic motif appears on page 92. Transfer on to stencil card. Tape the stencil in place on the first corner.

2 Add a touch of yellow ochre artists' acrylic to white artists' acrylic to make a cream colour or use cream emulsion. Apply the paint through the stencil on the first corner using a small piece of foam rubber.

3 Continue moving the stencil around the chest of drawers until you have completed the four corners. Note how the border line connects.

4 Mark a centre line on each side of the chest of drawers lightly in pencil.

5 Tape the stencil into position and apply the paint as you have done on the front.

6 When the paint is dry, lightly sand the stencil pattern to soften its edges.

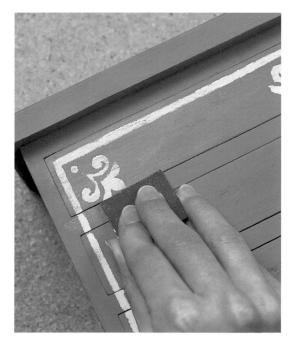

COTTON CURTAIN

MELANIE WILLIAMS

STENCILLING STRONG COLOURS and motifs on to very plain, inexpensive fabric is a great way to transform it into a striking tablecloth or curtain. This natural cotton fabric has been worked with a bold, graphic border made up from layers of simple shapes. The curtain is hung from easy-to-make loops.

Although templates appear on page 93 to enable you to replicate the pattern shown here, there is no reason why you should not draw inspiration from elsewhere and create your own motifs and images.

~

MATERIALS AND EQUIPMENT

- *lightweight cotton fabric to fit window area* • *stencil card*
- *fabric paints* • *natural sponge* • *coloured thread*
- *masking tape* • *iron*
- *sewing machine (optional)*
- *pins* • *tracing paper*
- *pencil* • *scalpel* • *palette or saucers*

. . . . . .

1 Trace the patterns on page 93 and transfer them to the stencil card. Cut out the stencils using a scalpel.

2 Mix up some yellow paint in a saucer. Secure the border stencil close to the edge of the fabric using strips of masking tape. Sponge the stencil with yellow and repeat around the edge of the fabric. Press with a warm iron when the paint is almost dry.

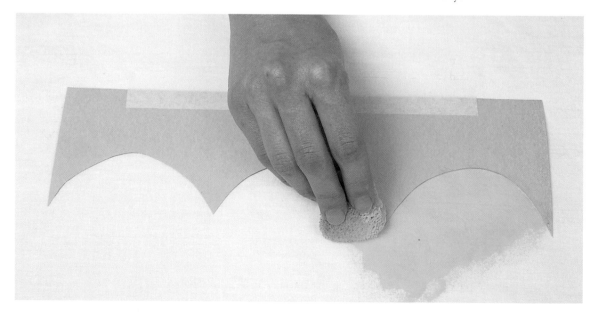

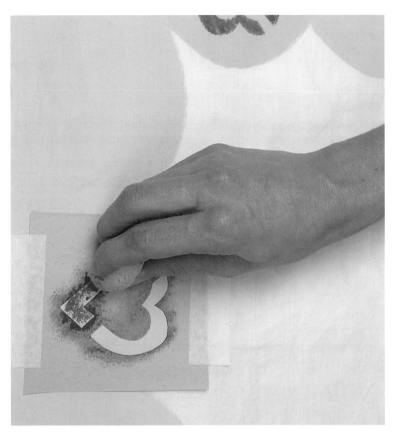

3 In another saucer, mix up a little red paint. Tape the heart stencil into one of the 'bumps' on the border and secure with tape. Sponge the heart with red, carefully lifting off the stencil and repeating the motif in every alternate 'bump'. Press with a warm iron when the paint is almost dry.

4 Mix up some blue paint and apply to the border edge stencil. Leave to dry then tape the dot stencil into one of the gaps between the hearts. Sponge the dot with blue, lift off and repeat around the border, filling in all the gaps to complete the design. Press with the iron once more.

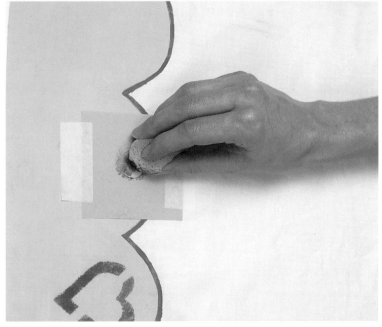

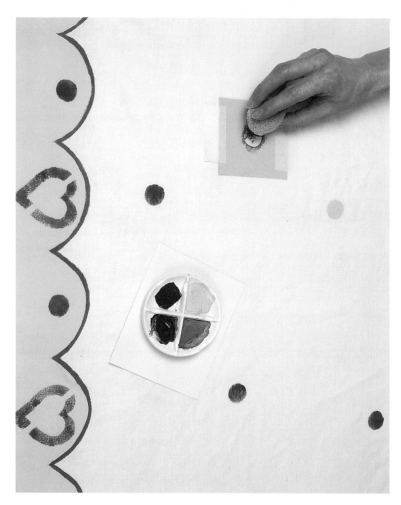

5 Use the same dot stencil to sponge red, yellow and blue paint over the curtain, wiping the stencil clean between applications. When you are pleased with the design, press the fabric with a warm iron.

6 Press a small double hem all round the curtain, pinning the hem in place as you go. Either stitch the hem by hand or, for speed, use a sewing machine.

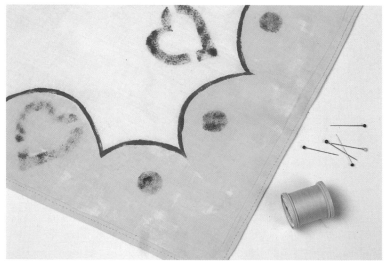

7 To make the hanging loops, cut the remaining fabric into 17 x 9 cm (6½ x 3½ in) strips. (You will not need many; for this small curtain, five loops were sufficient.) Fold each strip lengthwise, bringing both long sides into the centre. Press and fold in half lengthwise once more. Stitch along the side to secure it. Repeat this procedure for each loop.

8 Using a tape measure to help you, position the loops at equal distances along the top of the curtain, tuck under the raw edges and hand sew in place.

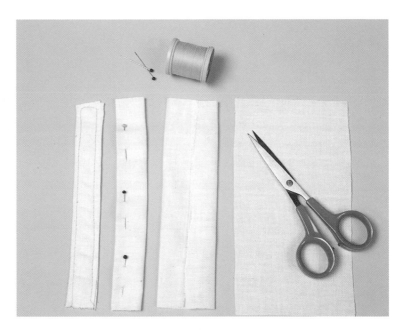

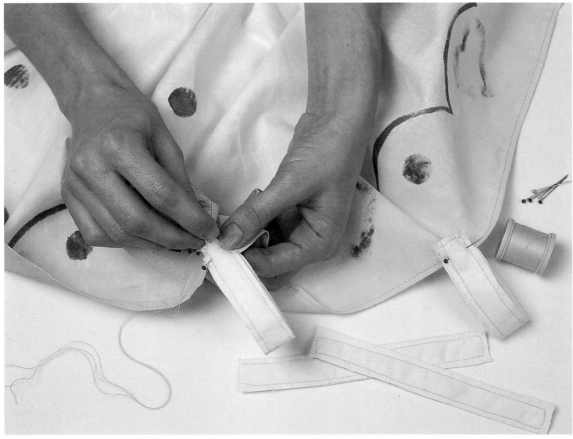

GARDEN TRUG

KATHY FILLION RITCHIE

A PLAIN GARDEN TRUG has been given a decorative stencilled border to transform it into a lively container for ornamental gourds, dried flowers or even freshly dug vegetables.

Although a folksy decoration in its own right, the trug makes an ideal gift for a gardening friend.

~

MATERIALS AND EQUIPMENT

● *tracing paper* ● *pencil* ● *cadmium deep red, hooker's green and white artists' acrylic* ● *stencil card* ● *scalpel* ● *pieces of foam rubber* ● *masking tape* ● *ruler or tape measure* ● *fine abrasive paper.*

. . . . . .

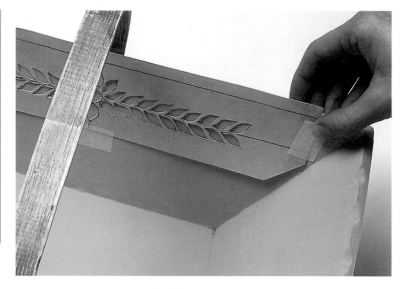

1 Transfer the patterns on page 93 on to stencil card and cut out in the usual way. Mark centre lines on the long inner edges and the short outer edges of the trug. Tape the stencil into position on these centre lines.

2 Start with the short outer edge, tape the stencil and apply the paint, beginning with the centre flower, using cadmium deep red mixed with a little green to give it a greyness.

3 Apply the paint to the leaves using hooker's green mixed with white to lighten it and a little red for greyness. You may chose to cover the flower pattern with masking tape to prevent you stencilling green over red or you can just carefully sponge around the flower avoiding the red.

4 Attach the stencil to the long inner edge and apply the paint in the same way as you did for the short outer edge. Remember to tape the stencil into place.

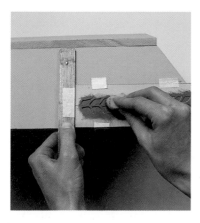

5 Tape the stencil in place on one side of the handle. Use masking tape over the handle to prevent getting paint on it. Apply the green paint through the stencil.

6 Flip the stencil over so that you are using the other side as a mirror image and paint the leaf pattern on the other side of the handle. When you have completed the stencilling you can lightly sand the stencil pattern to 'distress' it.

CERAMIC TILES

CHRIS FOX

LIVEN UP PLAIN glazed tiles in a kitchen or bathroom with this attractive Delft-style design. Ceramic paints are specially formulated for this type of decoration and come in a range of clear bright colours, offering you a choice if you wish to adapt this idea to suit your own decor.

Tiles must be clean, dry and free from grease and dust before the paint is applied. However, ceramic paints are for decorative use only and must be wiped over carefully when cleaned. As they take about four hours to dry, any disasters can be wiped off with soapy water and stencilled afresh.

~

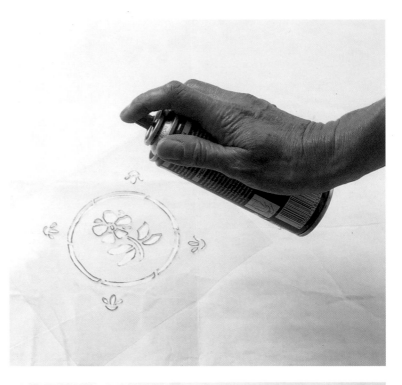

1 Use the motif on page 93 and enlarge or reduce it to fit your tile size. Using a waterproof pen, transfer the motif to a piece of acetate that is slightly larger than your tile. Cut the stencil with a sharp knife and lay it face down on a piece of scrap paper and spray the back with adhesive. Allow to dry for a few seconds.

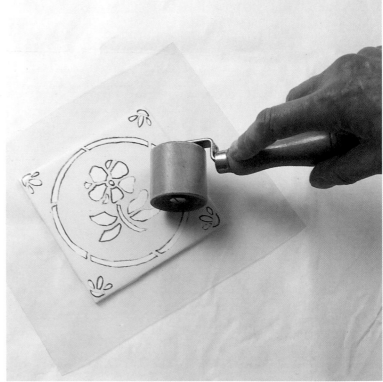

2 Position the stencil the right way up, centrally on the tile, and press it down firmly so that the paint will be unable to seep underneath. (A wallpaper seam roller is helpful to ensure good contact between stencil and tile.)

3 Pour some paint into a saucer, dip in the sponge and remove any excess by dabbing it on to some kitchen paper. Dab the paint through the stencil, being careful not to drag the sponge across it, and lose the dappled effect. If you want a strong colour, you may have to repeat the process.

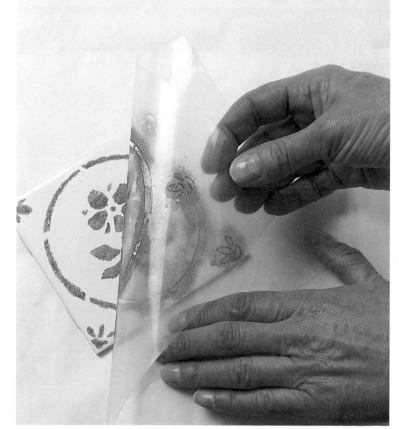

4 Hold down the stencil on one side while gently peeling it away from the other in order not to slide the stencil over the slippery surface of the tile and smudge the paint. Use the tip of a fine paintbrush if any soft edges need tidying up.

DADO RAIL

KATHY FILLION RITCHIE

INTERIOR ARCHITECTURAL details have become increasingly fashionable and rather popular. This ordinary dado rail has been given a stylish, classical look by stencilling it with an attractive leaf and berry design. Paint the rail with a white vinyl matt emulsion first to give a base coat to your pattern.

It is important on this type of stencilling to use registration and centring marks to align the pattern each time.

Use this design in other elements of the room, perhaps on scatter cushions or as a border to a plain curtain or tablecloth.

~

MATERIALS AND EQUIPMENT

- *tracing paper* • *artists' acrylics in chrome oxide green, turquoise, white, light yellow, yellow ochre, or matt emulsion in similar colours* • *gilt wax* • *ruler* • *pencil* • *stencil card* • *scalpel* • *masking tape* • *pieces of foam rubber* • *wire brush*
......

1 This stencil has a horizontal centring line and a vertical one which helps you later position the vein stencil and the berry stencil. Mark your lines lightly in pencil.

2 Transfer the patterns on page 93 on to stencil card and cut out in the usual way. Use masking tape to hold the stencil in place, positioning it on the centring marks.

3 This stencil is a combination of two colours, chrome oxide green and turquoise, which are blended together right through the stencil. Use a piece of foam rubber and apply the green first, leaving some areas of your leaves unpainted, ready for the blue.

4 Apply the gilt wax with your fingertip to add subtle highlights to the leaves.

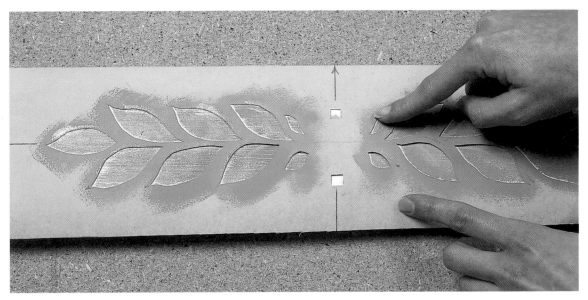

5 Position the vein stencil and
secure it with masking tape.
Apply a light green which is
made by adding more white to
the leaf green.

6 Position the berry stencil and secure with masking tape. Stencil in the berries in light yellow and a yellow ochre.

7 When the paint is thoroughly dry, brush it lightly with a wire brush, always working with the grain of the wood. This is a way to break up the pattern and add texture to the painted surface. Re-touch the leaves with gold highlights using gilt wax, where necessary.

PATTERNS

Wall Cabinet page 32

Use a photocopier to enlarge all
patterns on this page by 130%

Silk Scarf page 36

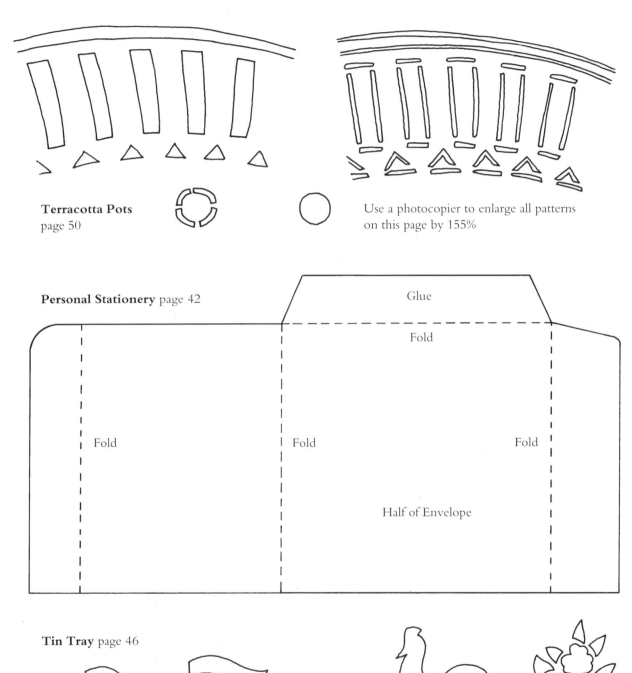

Terracotta Pots
page 50

Use a photocopier to enlarge all patterns
on this page by 155%

Personal Stationery page 42

Glue

Fold

Fold

Fold

Fold

Half of Envelope

Tin Tray page 46

Use a photocopier to enlarge these patterns by 240%

Floorcloth
page 54

Small Chest of Drawers
page 66

Use a photocopier to copy these patterns at the same size

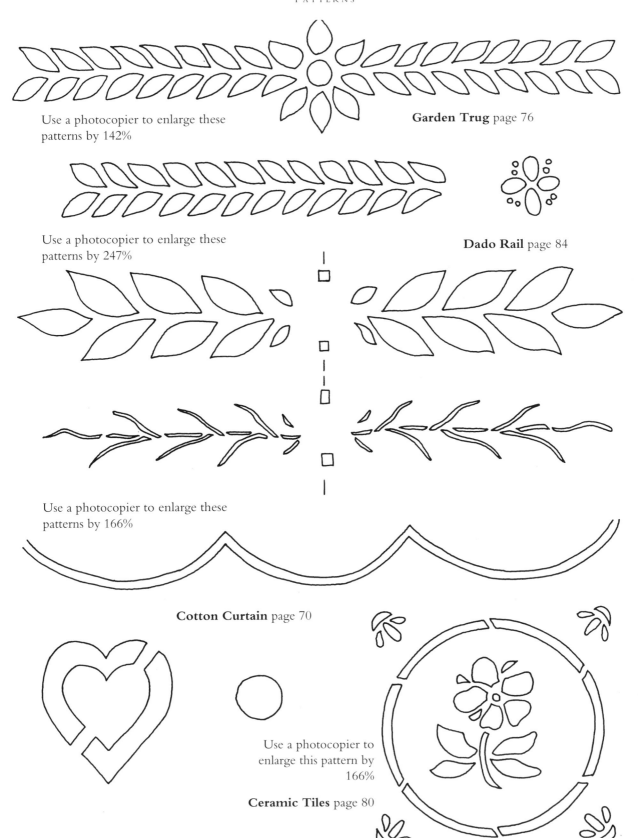

Use a photocopier to enlarge these
patterns by 142%

Garden Trug page 76

Use a photocopier to enlarge these
patterns by 247%

Dado Rail page 84

Use a photocopier to enlarge these
patterns by 166%

Cotton Curtain page 70

Use a photocopier to
enlarge this pattern by
166%

Ceramic Tiles page 80

SUPPLIERS

UNITED KINGDOM

MATERIALS AND EQUIPMENT SUPPLIERS

JW BOLLOM, 314 Old Brompton Road, London SW5 0BP Tel: 0171 370 3252

BRODIE AND MIDDLETON LTD, 68 Drury Lane, London WC2B 5SP Tel: 0171 836 3289

GEORGE ROWNEY AND CO LTD, 12 Percy Street, London W1A 2BP Tel: 0171 636 8241

GREEN & STONE, 259 King's Road, London SW3 5ER Tel: 0171 352 0837

PETER FISHER LTD, 16 Trongate, Glasgow G1 5EU Tel: 0141 552 0913/0710

COLE & SON LTD, PO Box 4BU, 18 Mortimer Street, London W1A 4BU Tel: 0171 370 3252

L CORNELISSON & SON LTD, 105 Great Russell Street, London WC1B 3RY Tel: 0181 636 1045

THOMAS KELLY & CO. (PAINTS AND PAPERS) LTD, 44-48 Dublin Road, Belfast Tel: 01232 320114

W HABBERLEY MEADOWS LTD, 5 Saxon Way, Chelmsley Wood, Birmingham B37 5AY Tel: 0121 770 2905

W J GARDNER (CARDIFF) LTD, 131-141 Crewys Road, Cathays, Cardiff CP2 4XY Tel: 01222 227631

CRAIG & ROSE, 172 Leith Walk, Edinburgh EH6 5EB Tel: 01315 541131

STENCIL DESIGNERS AND SUPPLIERS

LYN LE GRICE STENCIL DESIGN LTD, 53 Chapel Street, Penzance, Cornwall TR18 4AF Tel: 01736 69881/64193

THE STENCIL STORE, 20-21 Heronsgate Road, Chorleywood, Herts WD3 5BN Tel: 01923 285577

ELEANOR ALLITT, Thickthorn Cottage, 108 Leamington Road, Kenilworth, Warwickshire CV8 2AA Tel: 01926 52395

PROVIDENCE CABINETMAKERS, New Road, Barton, Cambridge CB3 7BD Tel/Fax: 01223 264666

UNITED STATES

PEARL PAINT COMPANY INC, 308 Canal Street, New York, NY 10013 Tel: 212 431-7932

CHARRETTE CORPORATION, 215 Lexington Avenue, New York, NY 10016 Tel: 212 683-882

JOHNSON PAINT COMPANY, 355 Newberry Street, Boston, Massachusetts 02115 Tel: 617 536-4244

THE STENCILER'S EMPORIUM, PO Box 6039, Hudson, Ohio 44236-6039 Tel: 216 656-2827

In the United States, a non-profit organization exists which is designed to help anyone interested in the art of stencilling. For information write to: Stencil Artisans League Inc, PO Box 920190, Norcross, Georgia 30092.

AUSTRALIA

ART SMART, 50 Ethel Street, Seaforth NSW 2092 Tel: 02 949 7477

OXFORD ART SUPPLIES, 221-223 Oxford Street, Darlinghurst NSW 2010

SPEEDY ART SUPPLIES, PO Box 151, Sunnybank, Queensland 4109 Tel: 07 208 0866

NEW ZEALAND

PARKING & PAYNE, 9 Spring Street, Onehunga, Auckland Tel: 09 636 5080

R L BUTTON & CO LTD, 8/38 Eaglehurst Road, Penrose Tel: 09 525 0535

INDEX